IDA

CERES

KLEOPATRA

VESTA

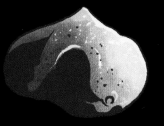

MATHILDE

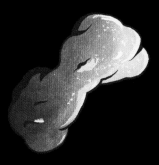

KLEOPATRA

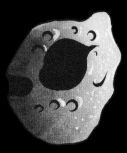

LUTETIA

BENNU

EROS

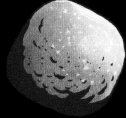

BENNU

IDA

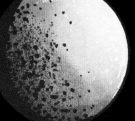

CERES

To Joan Kuchner
MJK

For Mom & Dad
MS

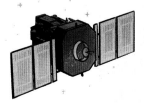

Acknowledgments

Marc J. Kuchner would like to thank Ralph Milliken and
Cody Schultz for their scientific expertise, Jermey Matthews
and Lisa Amstutz for believing in this project, and
Jennifer Nuzzo for her love and friendship.

MIT Kids Press, an imprint of Candlewick Press, 99 Dover Street, Somerville, Massachusetts 02144. mitkidspress.com candlewick.com

Printed in Shenzhen, Guangdong, China. 24 25 26 27 28 29 CCP 10 9 8 7 6 5 4 3 2 1

COSMIC COLLISIONS

ASTEROID

VS.

COMET

Dr. Marc J. Kuchner

illustrated by
Matt Schu

≡ mit Kids Press

We've got a marvelous matchup tonight, folks! A comet is speeding in from the outer solar system, and an asteroid is right in its path. Who will be left standing after this incredible interplanetary smackdown?

Comets speed around and around the Sun like trains on invisible tracks. A comet's invisible track is called an **orbit.**

VS.

THE CONTENDERS

In this corner: our asteroid! And he's looking . . . a little . . . out of shape.

Our asteroid is a lumpy fellow, sort of potato-shaped. He's a dull reddish gray and pockmarked with craters—scars where smaller asteroids have smacked him. Yup, this poor guy has already taken some punches. He must have something to prove tonight, folks. Can he see this through?

Asteroids are clumps of rock and metal orbiting the Sun that are too small to be called planets. They don't have tails, but many of them have funny shapes. Asteroid 216 Kleopatra is shaped like a dog bone.

In the opposite corner, over there by Venus: our comet, ready for ACTION!

Shining blue white! Spraying gas and dust! Sporting a glittering tail that stretches for millions of miles! He's a treat for your telescopes, folks. One big, bombastic COMET.

A **citizen scientist** is someone who volunteers to work on scientific research because of a deep interest in the subject.

And I'm your host.

I'm here to bring you the play-by-play, together with astronomers and citizen scientists from around the world who have been tracking these contenders for weeks.

Who will win this celestial slugfest? Who will survive this cosmic collision?

THE BATTLE ZONE

Keep your eyes on the asteroid belt!

Our asteroid has been training with about two million other asteroids in a part of outer space called the **asteroid belt**, or the **main belt**. That's where this battle is going down—in a busy neighborhood between the orbits of Mars and Jupiter.

Asteroids orbit the Sun just as comets do. Not all asteroids orbit in the asteroid belt. Some follow roughly the same orbit as the planet Jupiter. Others can be found near the Earth, close enough that we need to track them to find out if they might hit our planet!

Now don't blink, or you'll miss our Oort cloud opponent.

Our comet spends most of his time hiding out in a region called the **Oort cloud**, which surrounds the solar system. The Oort cloud is made of billions and billions of comets! But way out there, far beyond the orbit of Pluto, comets are too faint for astronomers to see, even with the biggest telescopes.

Not every comet lives in the Oort cloud. Some, like the Jupiter-family comets, spend most of their lives in the inner parts of the solar system.

While he was out in the Oort cloud, our comet orbited very slowly. Then, as he crept toward the Sun, he began to pick up speed like a ball rolling downhill. Now this natural athlete is barreling toward the inner region of the solar system, where he will zip through the asteroid belt and career around the Sun. If he survives his close encounter with the Sun, he's going to fly back out to the asteroid belt, where our asteroid orbits. This will be one for the history books, folks!

You would *not* want to be hit by an asteroid!

Potato-shaped or not, asteroids can really pack a punch. We know because every planet in the solar system has been beaned by hordes of them!

When an asteroid pummels the surface of a planet, the asteroid explodes and often leaves a hole, which people call a crater. Every year, many asteroids hit the Earth! Usually, the craters get erased by wind and water, but a few big ones have survived, like Meteor Crater in Arizona. Folks, that one is three-quarters of a mile (1,200 meters) across, the length of thirteen football fields.

A big asteroid hitting the Earth can really make a statement. It can fill our atmosphere with clouds of smoke and dust that last for years.

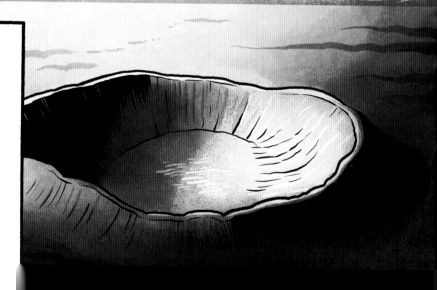

*An asteroid that collides with the Earth is called a **meteor**. Most meteors are small and burn up in the Earth's atmosphere. But some are big and sturdy enough to make it to the ground. When that happens, the piece that survives is called a **meteorite**.*

You would *not* want to get kicked by a comet!

When comets hit, they hit hard. That's easy to see because every planet in the solar system gets blasted by them!

KABOOM! In 1908, there was a huge explosion in the air over Siberia, Russia. Many scientists think it was a comet blowing up in the Earth's atmosphere. That cosmic wallop knocked down over a million trees!

In 1994, Comet Shoemaker–Levy 9 approached the planet Jupiter. Jupiter's strong gravity shredded it into at least twenty-one pieces, and all the pieces fell into Jupiter. For months, astronomers around the world watched tremendous plumes of white-hot gas rising up into Jupiter's atmosphere where the pieces had fallen. *BOOM! BLAM! Ka-RACK, ka-RACK, ka-RACK! BOOM!*

So where did these fighters come from, originally?

JUPITER

WHERE THEY FORMED

It started with a cloud of gas and dust . . .

Our asteroid, like all the asteroids in our solar system, formed four and a half billion years ago, in a cloud of gas and sandy dust grains. Those dust grains crashed into one another and melted together, becoming chunks of rock called **planetesimals**. Then some of those planetesimals crashed into one another, stuck together, and formed bigger objects—called **planets**.

The Earth also formed from colliding planetesimals—as did Mercury, Venus, and Mars. But our asteroid grew up a bit farther from the Sun than those planets did—closer to the orbit of Jupiter. He missed his chance to become part of a planet. You might say he's a leftover planetesimal that never grew up.

Disk-shaped clouds of gas and dust are seen around many nearby stars. Astronomers think that these disks are where planets, asteroids, and comets form.

Some of the gas froze!

The same giant cloud that formed the asteroids and all the planets stretched way out beyond the orbit of Pluto. It was so cold out there that some of the gas froze, covering the dust grains with ice. When those icy grains collided, they formed icy comets instead of rocky asteroids.

Many of those early comets crashed together and ended up inside planets. But not our comet! He passed near the planet Neptune one day, and Neptune's strong gravity flung him out into the Oort cloud.

Hold on, folks—I'm getting some important news!

This could be BIG.

Most of the comets we know about so far were discovered by citizen scientists looking at images taken by NASA's Solar and Heliospheric Observatory (SOHO) and Solar Terrestrial Relations Observatory (STEREO). These two spacecraft are always taking pictures in the Sun's direction.

Yes—it's really happening. NASA's SOHO mission has spotted our comet! SOHO's cameras are taking in new data as we speak.

Incredible! The new pictures show that the comet survived his close encounter with the Sun and took a sharp turn. He's going fast and heading for the asteroid belt. It looks like he's having fun out there.

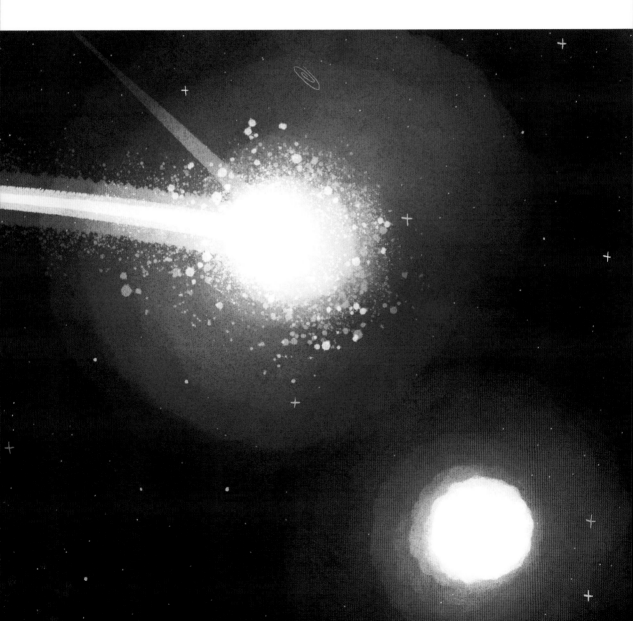

COLD VS. HOT

Our asteroid is chilly. Brrr!

Our asteroid is still minding his own business out there in the asteroid belt, coasting past Jupiter. And he's probably feeling pretty chilly. Asteroids in the asteroid belt are around -100 degrees Fahrenheit (-73 degrees Celsius). That's about as cold as the lowest temperature ever recorded outdoors on Earth!

JUPITER

The temperatures of the comet and the asteroid tell us how fast the atoms and molecules inside them are wiggling. The colder an object gets, the less its atoms jiggle around.

Our comet is SIZZLING.

Meanwhile, way out in the Oort cloud, comets can be as cold as -452 degrees Fahrenheit (-269 degrees Celsius). That's almost the coldest temperature possible (-459.67 degrees Fahrenheit)! But comets COOK when they fly near the Sun. A "sungrazing" comet, like Kirch's comet, can reach 4,900 degrees Fahrenheit (2,704 degrees Celsius). That's more than twice as hot as red-hot lava! Kids: NEVER touch a hot comet. Think about this matchup, folks. Does cold beat hot? Or does hot beat cold?

NOW LET'S TALK SPEED

That asteroid is moving well for a big guy.

Most main belt asteroids go around the Sun at speeds of about
11 miles (18 kilometers) per second. That's about five hundred
times faster than a cheetah can run! And a cheetah can run as fast
as a car on the highway. Yup, this warrior can really bob and weave.

Comet orbits are long, skinny *ellipses*. (An ellipse is an elongated circle–a kind of oval.) Because a comet's orbit is so long and skinny, it spends part of the time near the Sun and part of the time much farther from the Sun. When it is near the Sun, it moves extremely fast. When it is far from the Sun, it moves more slowly.

!!!

But that comet is in the best shape of his career!

Comets also go around the Sun. They always move faster than a train or a car, but when they get near the Sun, they get an extra burst of speed. A comet near the Sun can travel 60 miles (100 kilometers) in one second. That's 2,700 times faster than a cheetah. That's incredible, jaw-dropping, mind-blowing, bone-crushing speed! No wonder there is a DC Comics superhero named Comet.

There's just no denying that speed, folks. I bet you're ready to call this one for the comet.

Not so fast! Asteroids may not be as quick as comets, but what they lack in speed, they can make up for in size.

TIME FOR OUR WEIGH-IN!

Asteroids can be HEAVYWEIGHTS.

Asteroids come in many sizes. Most of them are too small and faint to see with the naked eye. However, big asteroids are bigger than the biggest comets. The largest known asteroid, Ceres, is 588 miles (946 kilometers) across, almost the size of France.

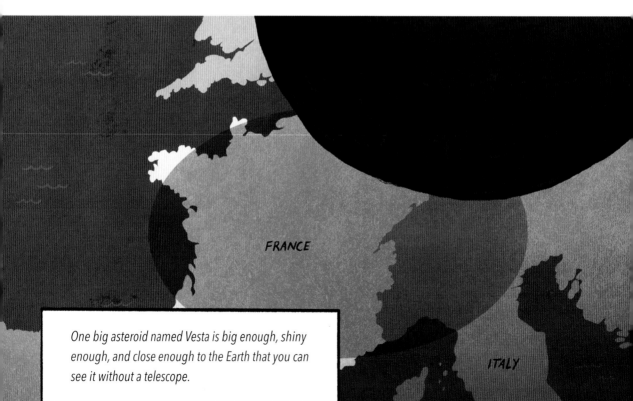

FRANCE

ITALY

SPAIN

One big asteroid named Vesta is big enough, shiny enough, and close enough to the Earth that you can see it without a telescope.

Comets don't get as big as asteroids.

The solid part of a comet, the nucleus, is relatively small. The largest known comet nucleus is about 80 miles (130 kilometers) across, a bit smaller than the state of Delaware. Comet tails can stretch for millions of miles! But most of that tail is just gas and dust that are released when the Sun heats the nucleus.

A big asteroid can be much bigger than the solid part of a comet. If our asteroid hits the comet on its tail, there won't be a collision! The asteroid will just breeze through that stuff and hardly even notice.

But it takes more than size to be a champion! Is our asteroid as tough as he is big? Who really has what it takes to win this showdown?

> *Did you know comet tails always point away from the Sun? They get pushed in that direction by sunlight and by the wind of particles that streams outward from the Sun at all times.*

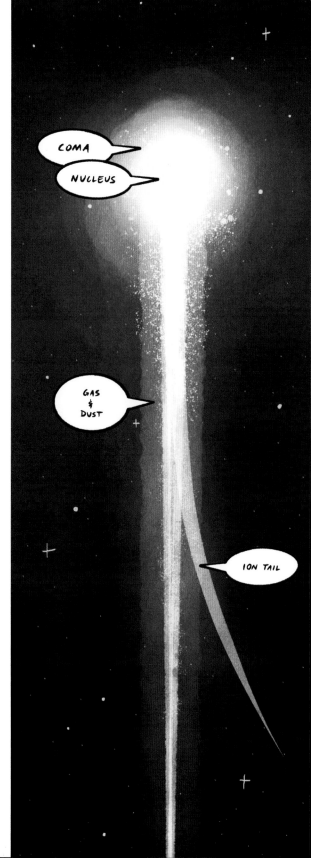

LET'S SEE WHAT THESE GUYS ARE MADE OF

Asteroids range from hefty heaps of rock to metal monsters.

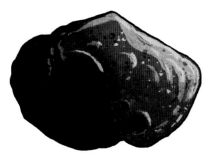

253 MATHILDE

Astronomers label different kinds of asteroids with different letters. C-type asteroids are the most common. These dark-colored asteroids are made of rock, clay, and carbon.

M-type asteroids appear to be made mostly of metals like iron and nickel. Nickel is a metal that is commonly mixed into steel to make it stronger!

21 LUTETIA

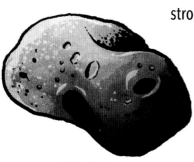

433 EROS

S-type asteroids are a mighty mix, combining both rock and metal.

Our asteroid comes from the inner part of the asteroid belt, so he's probably an S-type asteroid—full of metals like iron and nickel and tough rocks like basalt.

The S-type asteroid named Eros may contain 44,093 billion pounds (20,000 billion kilograms) of gold!

This comet, on the other hand, is more like a cow-burp Popsicle!

I'm not kidding. Comets are made of ice! Ice with bits of rock and dust mixed in. Some of the ice is frozen water, like the ice in your freezer. But the outer solar system is so cold that many other substances besides water can freeze into ice.

For example, comets can contain frozen methane and frozen carbon monoxide. We have these gases on Earth, too. Methane is a gas that comes out when cows burp. Carbon monoxide is found in truck exhaust. Blech! You wouldn't want a ball of frozen cow burp-truck belch slamming into you.

Scientists are always making guesses! When a scientist uses what we already know to guess what will happen in an experiment, the guess is called a **hypothesis**. A hypothesis is a guess you can test.

Well, now I'm thinking the odds favor that asteroid tonight since it's made of rocks and metal. Who's going to win? What's your guess?

FLUFFY OR TIGHTLY PACKED

Hold on! Don't guess yet!

What if those "rocks" that make up the asteroid are just in a loose pile? Could that comet bulldoze them away? Are comets more like solid ice cubes or stinky snow cones? If only we could poke an asteroid and a comet and find out . . .

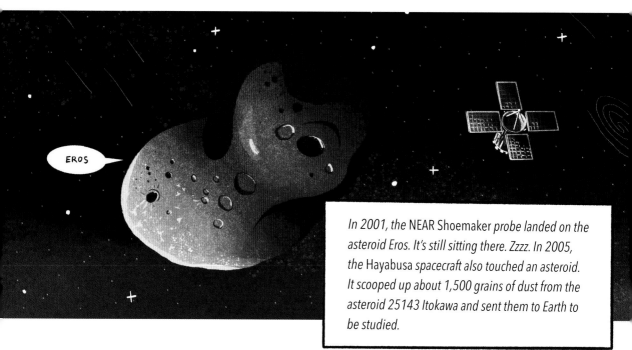

EROS

In 2001, the NEAR Shoemaker *probe landed on the asteroid Eros. It's still sitting there. Zzzz. In 2005, the* Hayabusa *spacecraft also touched an asteroid. It scooped up about 1,500 grains of dust from the asteroid 25143 Itokawa and sent them to Earth to be studied.*

Some asteroids are dense.

We can poke an asteroid. And we have! More than fifteen different space probes have visited asteroids.

Some asteroids turned out to be loose piles of rocks. But some turned out to be pretty sturdy. If you went to an asteroid, reached down and scooped up one cup of stuff, and brought the stuff back to Earth, it would probably weigh a bit more than a pound (a bit less than a kilogram). That's about as much as a can of beans.

Comets are weak and full of empty space.

In 2005, the *Deep Impact* space probe shot a disc of copper into the nucleus of a comet called Tempel 1 to find out what was inside. The disc was only about 3 feet (1 meter) across, but it left a crater 490 feet (150 meters) across on the comet's surface—about the size of a shopping mall! For comparison, imagine you kick a soccer ball onto the roof of a house and the whole house falls down. That's weak! One astronomer compared the comet to a bank of snow— mostly empty space.

   Our comet is closing in! Now it's only one million miles away from the asteroid . . . practically next door.

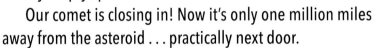

An object that is dense packs a lot of matter into a small space. For example, a cup full of water weighs much more than the same cup filled only with air because water is denser than air. If this book were made of iron instead of paper, it would be about seven times as dense.

DEEP IMPACT

COPPER DISC

TEMPEL 1

We're coming down the stretch, folks! Our comet is less than ten thousand miles from the asteroid now. Get those telescopes ready!

*Here's a hint: when two objects collide in outer space, it doesn't matter which looks like the fast one to us here on Earth, unless Earth is part of the collision! You have to stand on one of the objects (or picture yourself standing on one of the objects) and measure the speed of the other object from there. The speed you measure like that is called the **relative speed** of the two objects.*

Who's going to survive? What's your guess? What's your hypothesis?

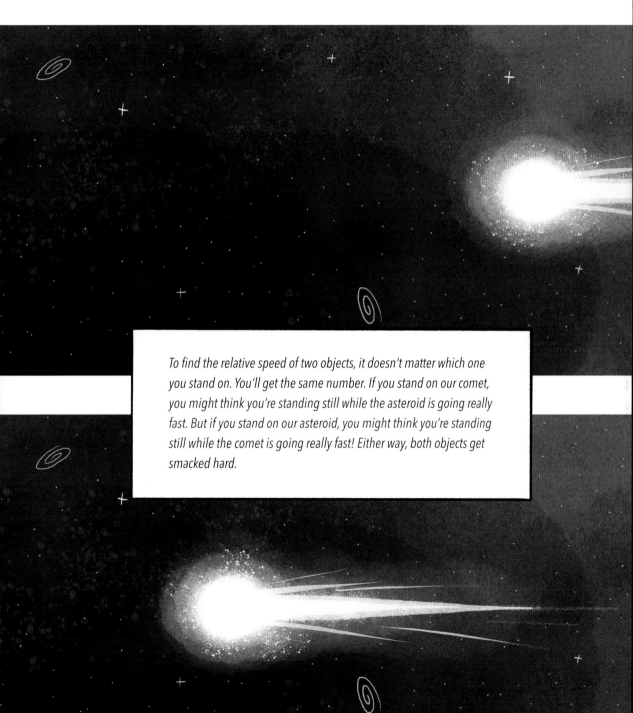

To find the relative speed of two objects, it doesn't matter which one you stand on. You'll get the same number. If you stand on our comet, you might think you're standing still while the asteroid is going really fast. But if you stand on our asteroid, you might think you're standing still while the comet is going really fast! Either way, both objects get smacked hard.

HERE IT COMES!

It looks like that comet's going to hit the asteroid any moment now.
Hang on to your seats, folks! It doesn't get any better than this!

What a sight to behold! We've got an enormous cloud of dust even brighter than the comet's tail!

Now let's check in with the amateur astronomers, the citizen scientists who've been tracking this comet, and get their take on this historic event. Say, could I get a peek through that telescope?

Sure, you can! We've been watching that comet for weeks. It was bright before, but nothing like this!

How bright would you say that cloud is?

It's even brighter than Sirius, the brightest star. I'd say it's about eighty times brighter than the comet was before the collision.

Incredible! There was no *bang* or *boom* when they hit. What's the story?

Well, there's no sound in space!

Of course! There's no air in space—nothing for sound to travel through!

Now, after that grand spectacle, we all want to know: Who survived this cosmic collision?

This just in, folks.

I'm getting the official word from the Minor Planet Center, which keeps track of all the asteroids and comets that have been discovered. They are telling me that the asteroid is still there! But he's not the same. His orbit has changed! And he's spinning more slowly than he used to.

The asteroid had quite a scare today, but he may keep fighting for billions of years. I guess he just wanted it more.

That brilliant comet is gone, taken out by a scruffy asteroid. Did you guess right? Was your hypothesis correct?

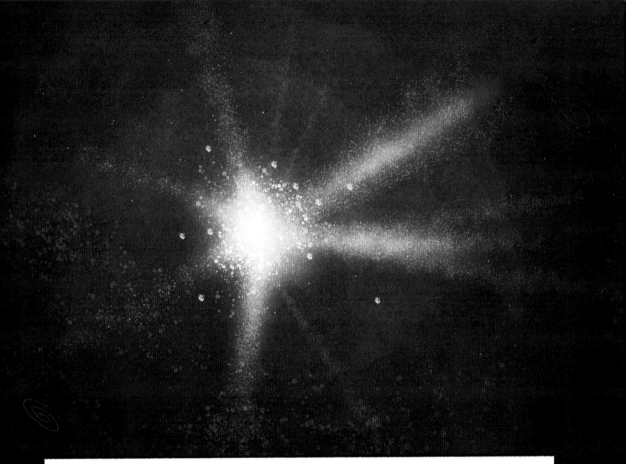

It's nighttime on only half of the Earth's surface at once—and one telescope can't look in all possible directions. So when a special event like a big collision happens, astronomers sometimes need to call up their friends on the other side of the world to get a picture.

Wait . . . there's more to this story.

TWO YEARS LATER

Hi, folks! Welcome back! Remember two years ago when a comet crashed into an asteroid, right here on our show? That colossal collision left behind a stream of small pebbles and dust stretching for hundreds of millions of miles across the solar system. Now the stream has reached Earth's orbit, and the Earth is passing through it on its way around the Sun.

That's right! Pebbles from the stream are zipping through our
atmosphere. Here comes a meteor—entering the sky near your home!
Wow! Look at that white-hot glow as it turns into gas.

You guessed it. That glowing ball of gas, once a tiny piece of our
comet, is what people call a shooting star.

Make a wish!

And tune in next time for more . . .

COSMIC COLLISIONS

FACT VS. FICTION

Have we ever seen a comet hit an asteroid? No. It doesn't happen very often; millions of years go by between major collisions between asteroids, between comets, and between asteroids and comets. Human beings have been around for only a few hundred thousand years.

So how do we know what would happen? We have never actually seen a comet hit an asteroid, so we don't know precisely what would happen. Also, our comet and our asteroid are made up! However, astronomers have seen a real comet hit Jupiter and multiple comets hit the Sun. We have seen how certain comets produce comet trails and how those trails produce shooting stars. Radar images reveal the shapes and sizes of comets and asteroids. Space probes have told us what chemicals some asteroids and comets are made of and how tough they are. Comets are small and fragile compared to asteroids. Comets sometimes even split apart by themselves as the Sun warms them—without being hit by anything other than sunlight.

When's the next time a comet will hit an asteroid? Can I watch?
Right now, it's too hard to predict when a comet might hit an asteroid. Astronomers haven't measured their orbits precisely enough—especially for the comets, whose orbits often change as they spray gas. But we *can* predict the next meteor shower, and you *can* see that! The American Meteor Society keeps a handy calendar of meteor showers at https://www.amsmeteors.org/meteor-showers/meteor -shower-calendar/. Next time one happens, head outside with a parent, friend, or guardian, find a dark place, and stare at the sky!

Can I really become a citizen scientist and discover my own comets and asteroids? Yes, you can! To learn more about the Sungrazer Project, the project that discovered most of the known comets, go to https://sungrazer.nrl.navy.mil/. There are also citizen science projects that will help you discover new asteroids. The International Astronomical Search Collaboration, at http://iasc.cosmosearch.org/,

has helped many teachers and students get involved in asteroid hunting. These projects are not limited to citizens or residents of any particular country.

Could I name my own asteroid or comet? Astronomers have an organization, called the International Astronomical Union (IAU), that assigns official names to stars, planets, dwarf planets, asteroids, and comets. The IAU traditionally gives each new comet a name that consists of the name of the person or the observatory that discovered it, plus an automatically generated code number. It's different for asteroids. The person who discovers an asteroid gets to propose a name for it, and if the IAU accepts the proposal, then that becomes the asteroid's official name.

Some asteroids have weird names! One asteroid is named Mr. Spock, in honor of a pet cat. Mr. Spock, the asteroid, is a reddish fellow about 13 miles (21 kilometers) across. You can find a list of asteroid and comet names at the IAU Minor Planet Center: https://minorplanetcenter.net/.

ASTEROIDS AND COMETS IN THE NEWS

Dwarf Planets

Have you heard of dwarf planets? Dwarf planets are the larger cousins of asteroids and comets. They are objects too small to be called planets but still big enough that gravity makes them round, like balls.

The nine or so known dwarf planets in the solar system live within clouds of asteroids and comet-like bodies. The first dwarf planet we discovered is Ceres, the largest asteroid in the main belt. The rest are out beyond Neptune, in and around a region called the **Kuiper Belt**. The Kuiper Belt is filled with icy comet-like bodies that sometimes turn into comets.

The dwarf planets Pluto and Ceres both used to be called planets! So was Vesta, the second-largest asteroid. When people stopped calling Pluto a planet in 2008, a lot of people got upset.

Interstellar Comets

Remember how fast our comet is? Well, most comets still slow down as they head out to the Oort cloud, and then they come tumbling back in toward the Sun.

But two recently discovered objects sped past the Earth so incredibly fast that astronomers realized they would never come back again! There is a limit to how fast an object can travel while remaining in orbit around a star or planet. The limit depends on how far away the object is from that star or planet. Objects moving faster than this limit don't come back for a second loop around—they just fly away. These objects, named 1I/'Oumuamua (pronounced "oh-MOO-ah-MOO-ah") and 2I/Borisov, are known as **interstellar comets** (or interstellar interlopers) because they are going faster than this speed limit for the Sun. Their home is interstellar space, the space between the stars.

These bizarre objects probably never orbited the Sun to begin with. They may have formed around another star.

The name 'Oumuamua *comes from a Hawaiian word that means* scout.
The name Borisov *is for citizen scientist Gennadiy Borisov, who discovered it.*

TEMPEL 1

HALLEY

'OUMUAMUA

BORRELLY